every day, i'll love you

by freya winters

this book is for:

____

a dedication to the person i love:

in the pages of this book, you hold not just a collection of words, but an insight into the depth of my feelings for you. it is dedicated to you, the most beautiful person to ever walk on this planet, and to the one who lights up my heart every day. i hope these pages serve as a reminder that you are so incredibly loved, cherished, and adored. as you journey through this book, please know that these words are but a drop in the ocean compared to how i actually feel about you. you have my heart forever, and please know that *every day, i'll love you.*

introduction:

this book is a compilation of love notes written for you to share with the person who holds the most special place in your heart.

each page invites you on a journey deep into the realms of affection, offering you a daily dose of affirmation for the extraordinary bond you both cherish. i understand that articulating the depth of your feelings can be challenging at times. that's precisely why i crafted this book – to provide you with words that mirror the immense love you hold for that special person.

although i've organized these messages as a daily collection, i want to emphasize that love follows no linear path. therefore, feel free to navigate through this book in a way that resonates with your heart.
it belongs to you and you alone.

consider it a beacon of affection, a testament to the love that defines your connection. what i really hope is that it fulfils your every need and serves as a constant reminder of the love that you both share.

freya x

to the one i love.

DAY #1

i hope you know just how important you are to me. i hope you know that there is no-one i would rather spend a day with. i hope you know how much happiness you bring me. i hope you know what a beautiful soul you truly are.

DAY #2

i'm proud of you for fighting the battles no-one knows about. for staying strong when you just wanted to give up. for remaining your true, authentic self when everything came crumbling down around you. i'm proud of you, in more ways than you'll ever know. you're my inspiration, and i mean that from the bottom of my heart.

DAY #3

every day i thank the universe for
blessing me with you. i am *so* lucky.

DAY #4

my heaven is lying on the couch, in your arms, dreaming about our future house, and all the little specific details. i *never* knew i would ever be with someone i could picture having a dream life with.

DAY #5

you made my dreams a reality the
second you told me you loved me.

DAY #6

it felt like it took an eternity to find you, but i'd
gladly relive it over and over again if it meant
i could spend the rest of my life loving your
radiant soul.

DAY #7

every single second of time spent with you is an absolute *dream.* even when you're taking too long to decide what snacks you want from the store, when you take ages to leave the house, and when you try and distract me from working.

you've completely and utterly illuminated my life.

DAY #8

with your love, i wake up every morning eager to celebrate life. the air that fills my lungs feels sweeter now, more refreshing, lighter, and nourishing. you've shown me that existence is beautiful, and that i deserve to experience this planet with *eternal* happiness in my heart.

DAY #9

trust me when i tell you that i have
never felt a love like this before.

DAY #10

i love talking to you.

the deep conversations, the silly chats, the quiet exchanges in the morning, the cozy late-night whispers...

i'll *never* tire of hearing what's on your mind.

DAY #11

thank you for sticking around when i've made it real difficult to do so.

thank you for being patient with me in the moments where i needed it the most.

thank you for making me laugh when all i wanted to do was hide away,

and thank you for loving the parts of me i've hated for so long.

thank you for helping me *heal.*

DAY #12

everyone has their unique motivation to get through
each day, and for me, all it takes is to see your face;
then, i'm ready to conquer the world.

DAY #13

meeting you added an entire spectrum
of color to my otherwise colorless life.

DAY #14

i promise to respect your boundaries.
i promise to give you space when you need it.
i promise to be honest with you at all times.
i promise to be patient and treat you with the respect
and kindness you deserve.
i promise to hold you tight and never let you go.
i promise to be your safe space, your sanctuary,
the one who shields you from life's harsh realities.

i promise to love you no matter what life throws at us.

DAY #15

when i look into your eyes, i can see our future.
i can see the love we are going to experience together.

i can tell that no matter what i'm feeling or how much i'm struggling, as long as i can look into your eyes, *everything* is going to be absolutely fine.

DAY #16

you'll never have to spend another
moment feeling unloved, *ever* again.

DAY #17

your love feels like those hazy summer days, when you have nothing to do but be out in the sunshine with the warm gentle breeze brushing across on your skin. it feels like freshly baked cookies out of the oven that have cooled down just the right amount, you know, when they're all soft and gooey on the inside? it feels like listening to your favorite song over and over again, getting goosebumps each time and never getting bored.

it just feels *right*.

DAY #18

you and me, becoming the best possible versions of ourselves, fulfilling our dreams, and absolutely flourishing together?

its a date.

DAY #19

if i could do it all over again, i'd meet you sooner.
i'd shield you from all the heartbreak.
i'd be the person you needed through the dark
periods of your life. but most of all, i'd love you the
way you should have *always* been loved.

that being said, i'm so grateful everything happened
as it did because here you are, with a special place
reserved in my heart, just for you.

DAY #20

the more time we spend together, the more i am certain you're the most perfect soul i have ever met. i just know at my core that you are the one person i will spend the rest of my life with. i love you *so* much.

DAY #21

i'll never give up on you.

DAY #22

as long as i'm still breathing, you'll
always have someone who is so proud
of you for everything you've achieved.

DAY #23

you're the love behind every single one of my decisions. you've grounded me, put me on the right track, and made me feel unconditionally loved every step of the way.

DAY #24

i know that my happily ever after
will always be with you.

DAY #25

all i can say is thank you for making me feel comfortable in my own skin. i never have to pretend or wear a mask around you, and i've never felt like this before. being with you has been the most freeing, healing, and *whole* experience of my life so far.

DAY #26

you make me want to choose joy.
gratitude.
happiness.
abundance.
nature.
new experiences.
an open-mind.
love.
life.

DAY #27

meeting you made me realize that love really does exist, and it exists in *abundance*. the love you give me is raw, unfiltered, and pure. its whole,

and it's all mine.

DAY #28

i'm over the moon to spend another
day under the same sky as you.

DAY #29

your inner and outer beauty is beyond my comprehension. you're *unreal.*

DAY #30

i'm thinking about you right now, and i can't stop.
i'm thinking about your kind heart, your loving eyes, and
your sanctuary of a smile. all i'm ever thinking about is
the countdown to being back in your arms again.

DAY #31

the way you look at me before you kiss me actually sends my heart into overdrive. i'll never get used to how incredibly beautiful you look in those moments.

DAY #32

days spent apart just don't feel right. there's an emptiness in my heart that can only be filled when you're by my side. no-one else even comes close.

DAY #33

you've taught me that love is not just a word;
it's safety.
it's patience.
it's unconditional kindness.
it's understanding.
it's communication.
it's the comfortable silences.
it's the little things we do for each other.
it's incredible.
it's so much more than i *ever* could have imagined.

DAY #34

i'm spending waaaaaaaaaaaaaaay too much time daydreaming about you recently, but i love it.

DAY #35

the truth is, you made me feel human again: an evolved, new, and improved version of myself. by simply loving me, you've lifted the burdens that once weighed so heavily on my shoulders. i've got a whole new outlook on life now, and it's all thanks to you. you've given me hope and a sense of belonging i haven't felt before.

i'm starting to enjoy life again.

DAY #36

you are my favorite place,
& i never want to be *anywhere* else.

DAY #37

i have never met anyone whose
heart is as beautiful as their face.

DAY #38

stop worrying about the way you're being perceived. no-one is judging you as hard and meticulously as you're judging yourself. you don't need to change a thing.

DAY #39

i'll do *everything* in my power to release the pain and suffering from your past and make sure that only beautiful things happen to you from here. i can't protect you from everything, but i'll do my best to make sure you're safe, forever.

DAY #40

the capacity at which you are able to
love has genuinely astounded me.
it's that fairytale type of feeling.
it's safe, it's secure, and it's *magic*.

DAY #41

i'll do everything in my power to make sure
life wraps around you as gently as possible,
easing your worries and making your time on
this planet as peaceful as it can be.

DAY #42

you make it easy to see the beauty in everything.

DAY #43

to be honest, you've completely blown my mind. well and truly. every day i wake up in utter disbelief when i remember that i'm the lucky one that gets to love you.

i'm the luckiest human to walk this earth.

DAY #44

please start giving yourself the love
you give so freely to everyone else.

DAY #45

the thing about us is, we just *click.* our relationship is the most relaxing, wholesome, fulfilling, and perfect connection i've ever experienced.

i honestly don't know what i did to get so lucky.

DAY #46

i now look at the heartbreak and sadness in my past as gentle nudges, re-directing me to you. you were worth every second i spent waiting for the right one, and i'd do it all over again if it meant i got to experience life with my soulmate by my side.

DAY #47

we're a power couple.
i'm so proud of us.
let's keep absolutely smashing life together.
i love you.

DAY #48

life is hard, but you make it so much easier. i just know that tackling hurdles with you by my side will make every challenge feel like an adventure worth embarking on.

DAY #49

there are so many people that want to see you succeed. never forget that there will always be someone cheering you on from the outside.

DAY #50

i just want you to know, it doesn't matter when
or where, i will always, ALWAYS, be there for you.

DAY #51

even in my wildest dreams i could never have
thought up someone as beautiful as you.

DAY #52

i love how we are the exact same kind of weird.
when we're together, we make the most mundane
of things exciting.

i love doing life with you.

DAY #53

i can't wait to experience life with you, savoring simple moments like watching the rain from our kitchen window and strolling through the park hand in hand. as we journey together, i know we'll create countless memories, and one day, we'll look back on our story and smile.

our adventures are just beginning.

DAY #54

watching you smile fills me with a love i never knew i was capable of feeling. *keep on smiling baby.*

DAY #55

you have made me believe in things i never thought
i could have. true love, soulmates, fate...

you have opened my eyes to a completely new
world, and what a beautiful world it is.

DAY #56

your heart is *golden.*

DAY #57

the grass is greener wherever you are.

DAY #58

you're good for my mental health.
for my nervous system.
for my thoughts, and for my emotions.
for my heart, and for my soul.

you're good for me.

DAY #59

you radiate the type of energy that illuminates not only the room but also the surrounding corridors, the kind of energy that leaves people feeling better after being in its presence.

you're beautiful - in more ways than the human eye can see.

DAY #60

at the core of it, you've made me
fall in love with life again,

DAY #61

you make me want to move through my fears, to tackle my demons, and to love my inner child to their core.

you've completely elevated my life.
you've changed me.

DAY #62

you have *everything* you need within
you to live the life you've always dreamed of.
i've never doubted you, not for one second.

DAY #63

me and you? it's a date. dancing in our kitchen at 3 in the morning, ordering takeout and putting our favorite movie on, going on rainy walks and coming home to fall asleep in eachothers arms, booking holidays to new places and exploring the world...

this is just the beginning.

DAY #64

the truth is,

you handle me better than i handle myself.

DAY #65

you radiate sunshine.
i'm ridiculously drawn to your energy.

DAY #66

when i'm with you,
my mind is quiet,
my thoughts are calm,
and my heart is *full*.

DAY #67

what sets you apart from the rest is your ability to love. to listen. to be patient, present, and loving during difficult conversations. to make me laugh when all i want to do is cry. but most of all, your ability to dream, to grow, and to heal no matter what life throws at you. you're a massive inspiration of mine, i learn so much about life just by being with you.

DAY #68

if only i could go back in time and show the younger version of me who i ended up falling in love with.

they'd be absolutely over the *moon.*

DAY #69

you just make existing so much easier. lighter. more enjoyable. life has become a pleasure to be a part of, and it's all because of you.

DAY #70

each moment we share feels like the
perfect chapter gracefully unfolding.

DAY #71

to say you are a dream come true would honestly
be the understatement of the century.

DAY #72

i'm yours.
now,
tomorrow,
forever.

there will never be a day when
i don't love you more than life itself.

DAY #73

i have looked at your face 5 million times,
but my heart still skips a beat when i see those
eyes. somehow,

i'm still getting *completely* lost in them.

DAY #74

we have the best kind of love. it's a love built on trust, respect, and a real, deep, authentic connection. we understand each other in ways that words can't always express. it's forever a source of strength and comfort, and something we can both rely on no matter what. our love is in the laughter we share, its in the dreams we create, and the warmth of our embrace. it's a love that somehow grows stronger each waking moment.

i love our love.

DAY #75

i knew it from the moment i saw your smile.
i knew it from the moment you told me you loved me. i knew it in the moments i caught myself smiling uncontrollably every time you crossed my mind. i knew it,

it's always been you.

DAY #76

you have made me feel something i never thought possible. you have made me feel a type of love i never thought i deserved. you make me feel warm, safe, and important. you make me feel like i can take on anything the world throws at me. *i've never felt like this before.*

DAY #77

i have faith that no matter
what unfolds in our lives,
our paths will *always* lead
us back to each other.

DAY #78

guess what?
i'm yours now,
and i'll be yours forever
if you'll let me.

DAY #79

i promise to love you with all the love i have.
i promise to spend my time thinking of new ways
to bring a smile to your face. i promise to make you
feel like the most important person on this planet.
i promise to hold you in the hard times, and the
good. i promise that no matter what happens, i will
always make you feel loved, cherished, and adored.

DAY #80

i still remember the butterflies i got when we first started talking. there's a reason why i remember them so vividly, and it's because i still get them to this day.

my excitement for you never really went away.

DAY #81

the thing about us is, we can talk to each other about anything and everything. it feels like we've known each other our whole lives, and no matter what the world throws at us, we will always be standing side by side through it all. with you, everything changes, and it changes for the better.

DAY #82

at the end of the day,

you are the person i want to come home to.

you are the person i want to cry to.

you are the person i want to look at as i drift off to sleep.

you're the person i want to hold in my arms through the difficult times.

you're the person for me.

DAY #83

you have taken away any fear, any doubt,
and any pain that my heart was holding on
to. i will never be able to thank you enough
for what you have done for me.

DAY #84

to put it simply, there's not
one part of you i don't want.

DAY #85

my mind is like a cinema,

and you're showing on every screen.

DAY #86

it's a connection beyond words, and there's no need for explanations because we're the only ones who need to understand. it transcends any language on this earth; it's an undeniable force. our silent understanding speaks volumes through the way we look at each other, laugh together, and navigate life side by side.

DAY #87

if i ever lost you, i'd be losing my: soulmate, best friend, happiness, smile, and reason to wake up everyday.

so it's probably best if that doesn't happen.

DAY #88

i never knew a feeling could reach so
deep into my soul until that moment
you smiled at me.

DAY #89

you're the comfort on my dark days, the sunshine on the brightest ones. you're my peace in the chaos, and the security amidst the sadness.

DAY #90

so many people enjoy being in your company. you'll never be able to see yourself the way everyone else does, but we all notice your beauty, your patience, your kindness, your aura, and your authenticity. you inspire so many people without realizing, and that's just one of the millions of reasons i adore you.

DAY #91

you make loving so easy. somehow, it is exciting, exhilarating, and non-stop, at the same time as being calm, silent, and solid. you're everything i could've ever dreamed of and so, *so* much more.

DAY #92

fyi;

i'm literally never not thinking about you.

DAY #93

i have a message for you:

i've loved you in the moments when you've hated yourself. i've loved you in the darkest corners of your heart, where you thought no one could ever reach. i've loved you through every heated discussion and every sleepless night. i've loved you forever and a day already, and every moment in-between.

DAY #94

if i could have anything on this earth right now, it would be me and you, cozied up in a warm blanket, with our favorite snacks, and the gentle rhythm of rain pouring down outside.

we'd have no obligations the next day, and we would stay up all night watching our favorite shows and only stopping to chat and cuddle.

i need this.

i need *you*.

DAY #95

i'm not just here for the good days and the pretty parts of you. i am here for the days when you can't get out of bed. i am here for the days you just can't manage a smile. i'll be here for you every single day, no matter what.

DAY #96

thank you for being
the calm in the storm
that is my mind.

DAY #97

i honestly couldn't ask for a healthier, happier, more complete, and fulfilling relationship if i tried. this is as good as it gets, and i'm gonna savor every single second of it.

this love is *special.*

DAY #98

you are my safe haven, my sanctuary,
the place where i find peace and solace.

DAY #99

i never knew my heart
was missing a piece of itself,
until you came along.

DAY #100

i'm yours. 1000000000000000000000% yours.
you've completely and utterly blown me away.
i genuinely didn't think it was possible for people to be
this good, and yet here i am, absolutely head over heels
for the most incredible human to walk this earth

i feel like i've hit the jackpot.

DAY #101

my love for you is the
one thing in this life
i'll never doubt.

DAY #102

you bring out the vulnerable
side of me i've tried to hide for so long.

DAY #103

not only did i love you from the beginning, but i'm falling even harder for the person you're growing to become. when i think about how much you're flourishing, it gives me goosebumps. you know your worth, and you're consistently striving for more. you're the most down to earth, authentic, inspirational person i've ever met.

DAY #104

this love is healthy. it's calm.
it's patient. it's whole.
it's kind. it's understanding.
it's everything anyone could ever want.

DAY #105

i just want to remind you that everything is going to be ok. it's all going to work out for you. the worries that cloud your mind will dissipate, and one day you'll wake up feeling lighter. and until then, i'll be right by your side to lighten the load. the sadness you feel isn't forever.

i've got you.

DAY #106

i'm still as obsessed with you as the day i first laid eyes on you. i'm obsessed, not in a neurotic way, but in a healthy, whole, and real way. you're my everything.

DAY #107

some of my favorite times have been just laying in bed with you for hours, talking about nothing at all, but everything at the same time. i love those moments with my whole heart.

DAY #108

the world seems so much quieter,
kinder, and gentler when you're holding my hand.

DAY #109

this is just a quick reminder that you are the most incredible person i have ever met and i will love you until the end of time.

you deserve to have an amazing day today.

DAY #110

i'm just so excited for the little things. waking up and hearing you sing in the shower. checking out cute coffee shops hand in hand. going for rainy walks and coming back to our cozy home. bbq's in our garden on a warm summer's evening. falling asleep on the sofa until 3 am, and stumbling back into bed knowing we get to lie in the next day. i think about our life together every day, and i get butterflies in abundance. our life is going to be beautiful. and you know why i know that?

because our love already is.

DAY #111

not only will you never be able to
comprehend my love for you

- but neither will i.

DAY #112

you bring out the side in me i've longed for, for what feels like an *eternity*. you've not only discovered the hidden door in my heart, but i've never trusted someone with that secret key as completely as i trust you.

DAY #113

the thing about you is, you're patient even when you're having a bad day. you bring your own light into the world even when you're feeling under the weather. your energy is unmatched. thank you for the laughs, the smiles, and the butterflies.

thank you for *everything*.

DAY #114

i finally found my place in the world.

it's with *you*.

DAY #115

our first home is going to be our safe space.
it's gonna be cozy, warm, and welcoming.
when we lock the doors and turn the lamps on
at night, we're going to feel like we're in our own
little bubble. our house will be filled with our
love for each other, happy memories, and so many
laughs. *just you and i.*

DAY #116

we don't argue, we communicate and gain perspective. we're not passive-aggressive, we speak openly and seek understanding. our relationship is built on trust, respect, and a commitment to growing together. it's an unbreakable bond. i'm so proud of us.

DAY #117

there's an infinite amount of beauty in the world, and i'll do everything i can to make sure you get to see every single little bit of it. i'll help you to see the sunshine on the darkest days. i'll take you to places you can't even comprehend right now. i'm going to do everything in my power to make your time on this planet as perfect as it can get. you deserve the *best*.

DAY #118

being without you makes me homesick.

DAY #119

falling in love with you resulted
in me falling in love with being
alive, and that is the biggest gift
that can ever be given.

DAY #120

i want you, i want all of you. i want you when you're happy, and when you're sad. i want to wake up next to you every morning and fall asleep with you every night. i want to stare at the stars with you and talk for hours about everything you've ever dreamed of doing. i want to travel around the world with your hand in mine, and i want to experience everything this life has to offer with you.

but most of all,
i want you,
and i want us.

forever.

DAY #121

you are the other half of me. the day we met was the day everything started to make sense. the pieces of my life finally started to fall into place. everything you do fills me with a joy i never knew i could feel, and i know that you are the person i want to spend the rest of my life with.

DAY #122

before you go to bed tonight i want you to read this:

you have no idea how many lives you've impacted just by existing. you don't always see the smile on people's faces after they've been in your company. you don't see how your energy impacts a difficult situation. you're not weak for crying, and you're not a failure for ever failing or making a mistake. at the core of your soul, you're completely wonderful. please promise me you won't ever forget that.

DAY #123

i promise to carry your heart with tenderness,
patience, and understanding at all times.

your love is safe with me.

DAY #124

thank you for always being there at the exact time i need you. thank you for always making me feel like i deserve to be loved. thank you for the endless support you give me. thank you for being the light in my life that i needed so badly. i love you an incomprehensible amount.

DAY #125

please don't ever feel alone. i want to remind you that no matter what, i will be here to listen to you until the end of time. it doesn't matter where we are or what we're doing, i'm always going to be here for you. this love is forever.

i'm not going *anywhere.*

DAY #126

no matter how far apart we are from each other,
always know that you have a piece of my heart with you.

DAY #127

you hold space in my heart
that no-one else could ever fill.

DAY #128

i can't wait for the late night giggles. i can't wait for the first time we walk into our new home together. i can't wait to eat chinese takeout with you while planning our next holiday. i can't wait for your face to be the very first thing i see every day. i can't wait for the rest of our lives.

DAY #129

i can't fix everything for you, but what I can do is make sure you never have to face anything alone.

DAY #130

your presence is magnetic.
your energy is magic.
your heart is enchanting.
your smile heals the parts of my
soul i thought i couldn't touch.
you are *perfection.*

DAY #131

it's a little embarrassing but,

i get really disappointed when
i get a message and it's not from you.

DAY #132

you're my favorite smile.
my favorite voice.
my favorite face.
my favorite person.

DAY #133

i wish you could see the stupid
grin on my face every time i think of you.

DAY #134

always remember i'll be by your side through everything life can throw at you. always remember that you deserve the world. always remember that you could not possibly be more loved. always remember that no matter how lost you might feel, i'll always find you again.

DAY #135

i believe that, regardless of when or where, in another existence or on a different plane, you and i will always belong together, side by side, hand in hand, *until the end of time.*

DAY #136

as long as i'm with you,
i'll always be home.

DAY #137

you are the reason i know what love is.

DAY #138

i'd pay an infinite amount of money for you to spend 1 minute looking at yourself through my eyes. perhaps then, you'd truly see just how incredible you are.

DAY #139

you are the safe haven my
mind goes to when the
world gets too loud.

DAY #140

i always thought i understood what true beauty was,

but then i saw *you*.

DAY #141

you are my paradise.

i never want to be *anywhere* else.

DAY #142

you were the best plot twist i could've ever asked for.

DAY #143

in the healthiest way possible,

i'm addicted to you.

DAY #144

you can turn my worst day
into my favorite memory.

DAY #145

when i tell you i adore you, i really mean that i *adore* you. every single part of you. from your deepest darkest secrets right through to your dimples when you smile.

DAY #146

for the first time in my life, i feel safe to be my real, true, authentic self. your love is the safe space my heart has been craving since i entered this world.

for the first time in what feels like forever,

i feel like me.

DAY #147

this the type of love that makes me want to chase my dreams, smash my goals, and grow my mind. you make me want to be a better person every single day, and that's one of the millions of reasons i know that i want to spend the rest of my life loving you.

DAY #148

you've ignited something inside me that hasn't awakened before. i'm getting glimmers of the new person i always wanted to be but had no idea how to get there.

DAY #149

you turn the most mundane
aspects of life into *magic.*

DAY #150

i know i could never love you more
than i do right now,

but tomorrow,
i somehow will.

DAY #151

wherever i am in the world, as long as i'm with you,
i know i'm right where i'm supposed to be.

DAY #152

you have inspired a depth of love
within me i never knew existed
before i saw your face.

DAY #153

when i look into your eyes, i discover a world i never knew existed—a world where i feel safe, cherished, and loved to my core. your ability to dissolve my worries is a gift i'll *forever* treasure.

DAY #154

we're gonna break generational curses.
we're gonna grow beyond our wildest dreams.
we're gonna expand our minds and open our hearts.
we're gonna absolutely *flourish*,
and do you want to know what the best part of it all is?

we're gonna do it all, *together*.

DAY #155

what made me fall in love with you?
your authenticity. your imperfections. your laugh.
your smile. your eyes. your heart. your honesty.
kindness. self-awareness. growth. emotional
maturity. your dreams. your goals. your *soul*.

DAY #156

i promise you that i'll always be there to wipe your tears. to give advice when you want it, and to hug you when you need safety. to buy you snacks when you're hangry, and to stroke your hair until you fall asleep. i'm your person, and i want to make sure your time on this planet is as perfect as it can be.

DAY #157

the love i have for you feels like breathing.
it is so natural, i can't believe there was ever a time
you were not in my life.

DAY #158

nothing, absolutely nothing could've prepared me for the amount of love i was about to experience, for the emotions i was about to feel, and for the smile that i'd be wearing 24/7. i've never met anyone quite like you.

what an honor it is to hold your hand in mine.

DAY #159

i'll always make you feel like the only person in the world. i'll always be your number one fan. i'll always be there to pick up the pieces when you feel broken. i'll always love you, and it'll always be an unconditional type of love.

DAY #160

every time i laugh, i'm thinking of you. every time i see something beautiful, i'm thinking of you. every time i stare out the window and imagine what my life will be like in the years to come, i'm thinking of you. not a moment goes by when you're not on my mind, and i wouldn't have it any other way.

DAY #161

honestly?

you stole my heart the very moment
i laid my eyes on you.

DAY #162

i can't believe i found my soulmate. sometimes, when i see your face, it feels like i'm dreaming. but the happiness i feel when i realize it's real is beyond words.

DAY #163

i'm not just attracted to the way you look, but i'm attracted to your mind. your personality. your heart. your soul. the way you interact with people. your open-mindedness. the depth of your character.

you're absolutely *extraordinary*.

DAY #164

together, we have a lifetime of sunrises
and sunsets ahead of us,

and we're only just getting started.

DAY #165

i love how we communicate. you respect me, and i respect you. we listen to eachother, and we really listen. nothing feels like an issue with you.

DAY #166

you are enough.
you are worthy of the perfect life.
you are deserving of *all* the love the world has to offer.

DAY #167

forever just isn't long enough to be with you.

DAY #168

i can't help but keep falling in love with you over and over

and over again.

DAY #169

from the moment you walked into my life,
my heart found its forever home in yours.

DAY #170

it wouldn't matter how long or how far i could search.
i would *never* find anyone as perfect as you.

DAY #171

your love made me feel welcomed, heard, seen, acknowledged, and supported, and that is one of the best gifts you could've ever given.

DAY #172

when we're apart, it's not just you that i miss;
it's your presence, your soul, and your essence
that i long for.

DAY #173

i want you to remember this:

i'm not giving up on you

i'll never give up on us. what we have is a special, next level, real, and pure connection.

not in my wildest dreams would i ever just throw that away.

you're my entire world and more.

i love us.

DAY #174

this is a short message to the person who stole my heart -
i will never stop loving you.

that is all.

DAY #175

one of my favorite things about love is the casual intimacy. it's in the way we hold each other's hands while having dinner, the sneaky grins we exchange when we're the only ones who have noticed something funny, the tender kisses planted on your forehead before falling asleep, and the reassuring hand on the thigh while driving. these are the small moments that speak volumes.

DAY #176

the best day of my life was the
day our hearts crossed paths.

DAY #177

being with you is like being in a dream i never want to wake up from. and the best part of that is that it's actually not a dream, our love is real, and it's *forever*.

DAY #178

somehow, i still feel the same way i
did when i first laid my eyes on you.

completely overwhelmed with love.

DAY #179

you are the kindest, most compassionate,
incredible person i have ever met. your strength
amazes me every single day, and i am in awe of how
you hold yourself during difficult times.
you deserve eternal happiness.
you deserve your dreams to come true.
you deserve the world.

DAY #180

you silence the noise in my head and give me peace. you make every day an adventure. you overwhelm me with the type of love i never knew existed.

you are my other half.

my happy place.

thank you for taking this journey of love. however you decide to use this book, i hope it has acted as a strong reminder of the passion and affection within your life.

i wish a lifetime of happiness, warmth, and love for you.

if you liked this book, please consider checking out my social media accounts:

tiktok: @everydayillloveyou
instagram: @freyawinters_, & @everydayillloveyou

Made in the USA
Coppell, TX
26 August 2024

36437660R00114